TOR BAY

**The history and wildlife
of Torbay's dramatic shoreline**

A celebration of the bay for the new Millennium

TOR BAY

The history and wildlife
of Torbay's dramatic shoreline

By NICK PANNELL

First published in 1998 by Nick Pannell,
27 Waterleat Avenue, Paignton, Devon

Printed by The Devonshire Press Ltd,
Barton Road, Torquay

ISBN 0 9533751 0 2

■ Front cover picture: Torquay's Natural Arch
■ Back cover picture: bottle nosed dolphins off
Roundham Head, Paignton

CONTENTS

■ An easterly gale in Torbay can have severe consequences for the seafront areas particularly at high tide. In February 1969 huge seas swamped Torquay's defences flooding Torre Abbey Meadows.

INTRODUCTION

THE COASTLINE of Torbay stretches for 15 fascinating miles from the gentle slope of Hopes Nose to the buttress of Berry Head.

Between these two promontories lies a richness of wildlife, landscape and history unrivalled on the South West peninsula.

On calm days a distant view of Torbay is hardly an absorbing one.

But get close to the water and explore its cliffs and coves, islands and rockpools and this blue-grey background reveals intriguing colour.

From childhood days when I first toddled to the water's edge and looked out over the turning swell it has held my gaze. Like a fan I have collected its memorabilia and followed wherever it has led.

Adulthood has not diminished my affection and I spend hundreds of hours every year enjoying the bay's sheltered waters, fishing, sailing or just walking the strand.

This book is a celebration of this love-affair as well as a guide to what the seashore explorer might hope to find along the rambling miles of Torbay coast.

At times we can only speculate as to what has come and gone. The land preserves its history in noble ruin. The sea allows no such record. Little of what has come ashore survives the constant tumult and is invariably ground to oblivion on rocks or sunk irretrievably in the sand.

The shallows hide their secrets but thanks to divers we know something of what lies rusting or mouldering beneath the waves.

Many of the photographs which illustrate the book were taken in the summer of 1927 by Paignton photographer Samuel Ensor.

They are from a fascinating collection discovered in 1994 in his former home. There were seven volumes, carefully captioned, and they provide a fascinating snapshot of life in the resort between the wars.

Lovers of the seashore will have explored for themselves some of the corrugated coastline between Hopes Nose and Berry Head. Ensor knew it well and captured the unchanging views. The full collection is now on view at the Torquay Museum.

I am indebted also to Torquay Museum for the use of pictures from the Tully collection and many local people who have provided information for this book including Dave Hardy, Ernie Tucker, John Pentney, Dickie Cord, Brian Murch, Nigel Smallbones, Brendan Jaffa and other member of the Torbay British Sub Aqua Club.

Finally to my friends and colleagues at Torquay's Herald Express for their advice and encouragement.

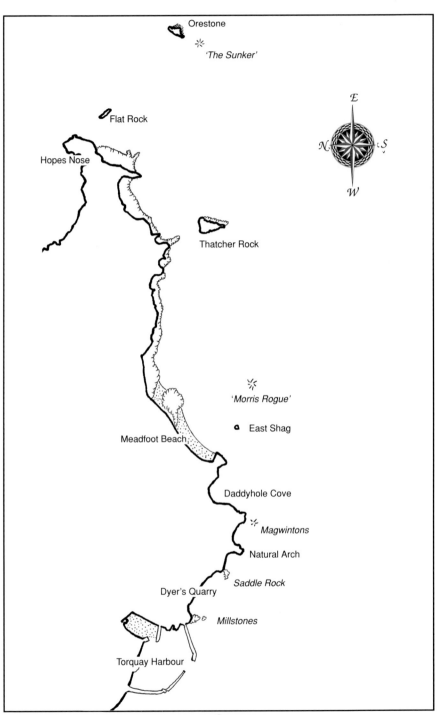

Orestone

'The Sunker'

Flat Rock

Hopes Nose

Thatcher Rock

'Morris Rogue'

East Shag

Meadfoot Beach

Daddyhole Cove

Magwintons

Natural Arch

Saddle Rock

Dyer's Quarry

Millstones

Torquay Harbour

E

N ❀ *S*

W

A PATTERN OF ISLANDS

Orestone, Thatcher Rock and Hopes Nose

THE ORESTONE is the easternmost of Torbay's two islands, a tight fist of rock which the sea has never quite prised open.

It lies about half a mile offshore rising suddenly from deep water to form an impressive citadel which even at the height of an easterly gale resists all efforts of wind and spray to overwhelm it.

This is no ordinary rock.

Paddle close and you will see how the strata is twisted into a stoney knock by geological forces. While softer rock unravelled around it the Orestone was left the indomitable fortress we see today resistant to all that nature can throw against it.

Approach the island from landward and you reach a battlement patrolled by black capped cormorants and crested shags. Its turrets provide kittiwakes with one of their most important nest sites shared by greedy herring gulls and their menacing black-backed cousins.

It's a noisy crowded place where every pitch is fought for and the displaced yell their indignation.

At low tide a small boat can drift in to the very base of the rock where the swell shoulders through thick kelp. Here the falling water reveals a dripping sea cave into which a skillful boatman can paddle on a calm day if not deterred by tentacles of oarweed which reach out across the entrance.

Inside the walls seem to breath as the swells rise and fall flushing the thirsty barnacles and sponges which adorn them.

There is further interest at the southern end where the battlement is broken by a steep incline and the sea has driven a narrow tunnel through the limestone heart of the rock.

On low Spring tides daylight can be glimpsed through the dark foundations and the passage is just wide enough for divers to swim through.

It is a tight squeeze, hindered by thick kelp and a rolling swell which gurgles through the passage on all but the calmest of days. The tunnel is also the supposed haunt of an outsized lobster which has deterred at least one diver from ever attempting the passage again!

Lobsters grow to about 15lbs and up to three feet long but can seem much larger to the diver when magnified under water. Many older specimens become encrusted with barnacles and the limy tubes of serpulid worms and can have a fearsome appearance.

The sea has always been the

haunt of monsters, most of them imaginary, but imagination is sufficient to deter even the most gallant from venturing into dark underwater holes.

Remains of at least one other 'monster' have been found close to the Orestone.

A few years ago divers discovered a 12 foot long crocodile skeleton wedged in a gulley here - a creature more likely to have been raised in Paignton Zoo than the intemperate waters of Torbay!

The Orestone, like a planet, has its satellites - underwater reefs which reach up from the sandy bottom to provide marine life with cover and anchorage. Find such a rock, and there are many around the Orestone, and you discover a silent, slow moving city which is home to a myriad of species.

Before the advent of echo sounders fishermen would locate these marks by lining up fixes on prominent landmarks. The rising seabed was recorded with the help of a plumb line.

No such techniques are needed to find the nearest of the Orestone reefs, a pinnacle rock known as the Sunker.

At low water it breaks surface, a swirl of white water warning boatmen to steer well clear. On calm days you can approach this barnacled spike and watch the light dance amongst the kelp which covers it. Among the swaying fronds predators await their next meal.

To the east another pinnacle reaches towards the surface. This is Seagull Rock, lying slightly inshore of the Orestone and less of a hazard to shipping. Crab pots often mark the presence of this subterranean rock which rises 18 feet from the seabed

The Orestone's most distant satellite is Tucker Rock, a tide swept reef at the very limit of Torbay's inshore waters. From here the seabed drops away quickly to a deep plain of sand and mud, a monotony broken only by the occasional wartime shipwreck further offshore.

Tucker never uncovers and even at low water springs is a good 20 feet below the keel. It is home to many marine species drawn to the rich, shallow water habitat.

Such lonely stations at the very edge of the deep water attract less common species more often found mid-Channel.

Divers recently swam upon a six foot angler fish slumbering in a shingle groove carved around the base of the rock. This camouflaged bottom dweller is so-called because of the 'fishing rod' appendage it dangles above its giant mouth. Small fish are lured by the mesmeric movement of the rod within gobbling range. Like many flatfish it is a master of disguise and can change colour to blend perfectly with the sand and shingle over which it lies.

Divers see what swims around them. Anglers have no such advantage and are often left with a broken line when they hook the unexpected.

I remember one summer evening fishing in the deep water between the Orestone and Tucker Rock where the tide scours deep pits in the sea bed.

Ray often feed here and it was with some optimism that I baited with a generous fillet of mackerel and let it drop into the streaming tide hoping that the fresh scent would attract some hungry predator. I did not have to wait long. Within minutes a strong tug on the line heralded a dramatic struggle with some unseen heavyweight I could barely prize from the bottom.

There are stories of big skate in these waters as well as sting ray and turbot but whatever took my bait that day remains at liberty having carefully chewed through the 20lbs line!

Despite the apparent danger the Orestone represents to shipping there are few wrecks recorded here. To the east a small wooden trawler, the Anna Marie, sits rotting on the sea bed while closer in lies the wreckage of a landing craft. Little remains of the craft but the rifle ammunition it was carrying is still found by divers.

And there are other remnants of war buried in the sand. A single engined Lysander based at Harrabeer in West Devon crashed into the sea near the island in the 1940s. Extensive searches have so far only located its engine and an instrument panel and with the passing years little else is expected - such is the corrosive power of the sea in this exposed and shallow place.

Inshore lies Hopes Nose, that peculiar finger of land sadly more famous for its sewer than the unique geology which attracts many field study groups from around the country every year. The study of rock is not everyone's favourite hobby but

■ **Thatcher Rock, sculptured by the sea, is the most verdant Torbay island.**

there is one element guaranteed to capture everyone's imagination - GOLD!

Gold was discovered at Hopes Nose in 1922 following a similar discovery on the foreshore of Daddyhole Cove a few years earlier. An Australian miner recognised the similarity of the limestone to gold bearing rock in his own continent and soon located the gold flecked strata he was looking for. A syndicate was formed to investigate the Daddyhole strike but was found to be commercially unviable.

The Hopes Nose gold bearing strata is exposed in the rock platforms to the east - an intrusion of cream coloured calcite much excavated by souvenir hunters.

TORBAY'S most celebrated island is Thatcher Rock, a favourite of sightseers and photographers for generations.

It lends a romantic quality to the coastline, sun bleached limestone reaching up to jagged turrets while gentler slopes encourage gardens of purple flowered tree mallow and sea beet.

But the island has a malevolent side with sharp reefs extending from Thatcher Point waiting to impale the foolish or ambitious.

At night too the island's imposing silhouette can unnerve the imaginative, the sculptured limestone resembling strange birds - too big for cormorants or shags.

I have anchored here on winter nights waiting for conger eels to emerge from their hideaways to feed. This efficient predator grows to about 60lbs in these waters but much larger specimens inhabit sunken wrecks further offshore where the rusting superstructure

■ The pilot of this Hawker-Typhoon could have chosen a worse place to crash land when his engine failed over Torbay in 1942. Meadfoot Beach provided a relatively soft landing and he and the plane were recovered with few injuries. Fresh memorabilia from the crash was recovered in the 1970s.

provides an ideal home.

The largest eels are taken by commercial fishermen and can grow to over 200lbs. This is a matriarchal society - all the big eels are female.

Other species also feed in the shadow of Thatcher. In the summer bass arrive to gorge on sandeels and brit. They shoal in the tide rip that squeezes through Thatcher Gut - the reef which extends from Thatcher Point and almost closes on the island.

They used to come in their hundreds and fishermen made huge catches, but over fishing, particularly with the gill net, has decimated stocks and a bass fillet is now the most expensive to be found on the fishmonger's slab.

Anglers still persevere however, encouraged by memories of past success and when the conditions are right half a dozen boats will be found drifting through the Gut, delicate lines streaming forth.

Thatcher Rock rises from a much shallower seabed than the Orestone and is only just an island. On the lowest Spring tides it is possible to scramble across weed strewn rocks to within a hundred yards of the rock when only a narrow channel between the rock and the mainland is navigable.

The shallow water and plentiful sunlight nurtures a fabulous underwater garden much enjoyed by divers and snorkellers who can get access to the shoreline from Thatcher Point.

To the north there are mussel beds and in the Springtime an army of brittle stars invade the banks.Their fingers trail in the current like a waving sea of grass sifting the water for food.

Anemones bristle the banks battening on algae while predator starfish creep in slowly on their prey. The common starfish is a disgusting feeder squeezing its stomach inside living shellfish and digesting them.

Up until the turn of the century goats were brought to the island to feed on the sparse vegetation. Tree mallow flourishes on Thatcher Rock, the limestone soil and seabird manure ensuring rapid growth in the Spring.

During dry summers, however, Thatcher's green cloak rapidly browns and it must have been a regular task of boatmen to bring fresh fodder to these stranded grazers.

Today the rock is home only to hundreds of seabirds which constantly circle the lofty turrets.

Man has left his mark below the waves. At the island's southern end an encrusted iron cannon is all that is left of some long forgotten wreck. It could be from the Revenue cutter HMS Vigilant which sank near Torbay in 1819 but the conclusive evidence has long disappeared beneath the sand and mud.

More recently a shell was found in the vicinity and blown up by bomb disposal experts. Perhaps Thatcher Rock was used for target practice like other islands along the South West coast before their value as nest sites for sea birds was appreciated.

All is silent now save for the calling gulls and the murmuring currents which embrace this most verdant of Torbay's islands.

SAVAGE SHORE

Meadfoot to Beacon Cove

OUR journey of discovery now follows the shoreline eastwards towards Meadfoot Beach where the rampart of cliffs is broken and two valleys descend to the sea.

The landscape here is distinctly Mediterranean, holm oak covering the undercliff and smart villas making the most of spectacular views. One of Torbay's finest buildings the Hesketh Crescent nestles in the shallow coombe

This is my favourite beachcombing bay, a steep pebble ramp that at low tide trails into sand. Each tide brings more flotsam ashore and unearths new treasures among pebbles and shells freshly piled by the retreating sea.

Long hours can be enjoyed pottering along the shoreline here collecting fistfulls of coloured and intricate objects their origin and nature transformed by the grinding waves.

The variety of undersea life in the waters immediately offshore also guarantees a rich assortment of organic litter - sun bleached skeletons and skins, egg cases and seaweeds. There is human litter too, thankfully less revolting since the sewage screening plant at the back of the beach came on stream.

Amongst the tangle of seaweed you will find the cuttlefish shell, popular with bird owners and fun to carve with a pen knife. The live animal is more exciting and thrives in the shallows of Meadfoot Bay.

I accidentally caught one a few summers ago while fishing a few hundred yards out and brought it inboard to examine it more closely. Within moments it had squirted its ink sack into the bucket; underwater this confuses predators, throwing a murky cloud in their face. Romans and Greeks used to extract this ink for writing which must have left some letters smelling distinctly fishy!

The cuttlefish is a predator itself, snatching at shrimps and prawns with its sticky tentacles. The shell we find on the shoreline is the creature's buoyancy tank which allows it to swim at various depths in the same way as a submarine.

Their other remarkable feature is the ability to change colour in the most expressive manner, blushing, blanching and rippling like waves over sand.

After performing some of these tricks and keeping us entertained for a while we returned this wonderful creature to the sea.

If you ever find a plank of rotting wood on Meadfoot Beach, and after an easterly storm the ocean's debris is piled high along this stretch of coast, see if you can find any shipworms concealed within.

These grow to an enormous size, up to a foot long in these waters but up to five feet in the tropics. They have a huge appetite and not the kind of passengers you want to be carrying in your keel!

Many bugs, worms and grubs inhabit the strand line of seaweed and driftwood and you will not be the only one searching it. Turnstones, scurrying birds with red legs and dappled plumage will also be scavenging among the sea-tossed piles.

Meadfoot Beach is an artist's canvas in constant change. Each tide is like a fresh brushstroke re-shaping its colours and contours.

On gentle days the waves pile soft sand against the limestone embankment so it forms comfortable beds for sunbathers. But on a stormy day when the wind veers to the east, rollers will strip feet of shingle from the beach in hours.

Among the rivulets which emerge from the pebbles at low tide is a fresh water stream which, if sampled, is bitter to the taste. This is the source of small mineral water industry which flourished at Meadfoot Beach earlier this century.

Samples analysed at the time showed that water from the Spring contained similar minerals to those in the spa waters of Bath and Harrogate.

The stream's source beside the road was taken over by the local council and bottled to be sold as 'Torquay Natural Mineral Water'

AFTER Meadfoot the cliffs rise steeply to form the plateau of limestone known as Daddyhole Plain.

While similar formations around our shoreline seem stable, this outcrop hangs precariously over the sea threatening to roll boulders on passing boats. Daddyhole Cove is too tame a name for this chaos of rubble - locals call it Thunder Hole.

From the top of the cliff you can see a ridge of limestone that has been prised from the bedrock creating a deep chasm. The seaward view is even more spectacular with slabs of rock piled up like castle ruins.

It must have been a sudden event the night the seacave which carried this section of cliff collapsed. Cliff erosion around the Devon coast is a slow process but here the patient sea found a weakness and drove home its advantage.

The boulders that were flung into the sea have created an exciting underwater landscape. A forest of oarweed and thong weed festoon the rocks and colourful wrasse browse the limpets.

The wrasse is a scaly and inedible fish, qualities which have no doubt saved it from slaughter. It is not fished for commercially and anglers generally return them to the water.

As we move into deeper water the rocks give way to sand where flatfish lie half buried awaiting their next meal. Thunder Hole was once a boat dump and remains of old ships, scuppered by their owners, can be found here.

Further out to sea again we

encounter a new area of reefs.

The East Shag is the only one of the submerged pinnacles which breaks surface and, as its name suggests, is a popular perch for shags and cormorants drying their wings. Unlike other seabirds these glass-black predators have no water resistant oils in their feathers and regular drying is essential.

This pinnacle, which is very visible from the Paignton side of the bay, is also known as White Rock, a description associated perhaps, with other seabird habits!

A hundred yards to the South East is one of the most celebrated diving reefs in Torbay. It is called the Morris Rogue, a malevolent name for a garden of sealife which lies just a couple of fathom below the surface.

A mass of plumuse anemones throng the southern edge of the rock while white star anemones stud the descending walls. Here too are brightly coloured sponges sifting the current for nutrients.

Sponges are a favourite food for sea slugs and like other sea creatures which hug the rocky gullies, they have a clever ability to match their colour to their surroundings.

This rich oasis was all but choked a few years ago when beach feeding at Meadfoot blanketed the seabed in muddy sediment. Since then the marine life has recovered and the Morris

■ **Natural Arch pictured at the turn of the century and the site of some dramatic shipwrecks.**

Rogue now harbours species of national importance.

The water's edge between Thunder Hole and Saddle Rock is inaccessible from the shore although a pleasant cliff top walk between the Imperial Hotel and Daddyhole Plain provides tantalising glimpses. This stretch of coast is best appreciated by boat but beware the Magwintons – treacherous, off-shore rocks which hide just below the surface at half tide.

This is a dangerous coast. Crews driven ashore during easterly gales have little chance of scrambling to safety because of steep, slippery cliffs and over the years many lives have been lost here.

Such was the fate of the crew of the Duke of Marlborough wrecked just to the east of Natural Arch on October 11 1836. It was a harrowing tale.

In an attempt to escape the white water her crew cut the port shrouds of the mast so it fell against the cliff creating a primitive ladder. The mate and a crewman attempted the climb but they were thrown back on deck when a large wave shifted the vessel. The crewman was killed but the mate tried again and this time reached safety. None of the others would attempt the precarious lifeline, however, and all drowned when the ship sank.

Paddle into this shallow cove on a calm day and it is difficult to imagine the drama of that stormy night. But see how the cliffs rise smoothly from the water with barely a ledge of handhold to assist the struggling sailor and you might grasp something of the ordeal.

Explore further and a cave emerges that has been hollowed from the limestone cliff and where a small dinghy can nose in.

It is here where one would expect to find the timber of the old Duke driven like pit props into the back of the gully, but despite the best efforts of divers, here and elsewhere, the main wreck site remains elusive.

Shortly after the tragedy six of her cannon were raised and there are stories of other artifacts brought to the surface in more recent years. Ancient timber was found further out to sea in the early 80s but the final resting place of this unfortunate ship is still a mystery.

Natural Arch was the vicinity of another, more recent tragedy. It was the night of December 7 1959 and a south easterly had whipped the placid waters of the bay into a cauldron of white water. Struggling at anchor was the Dutch tug Cycloop with three barges in tow.

Coastguards had been keeping an eye on her but at 9.40 that night all four vessels began drifting toward the rocks. The skipper of the tug, realising that urgent action was needed if is he was to regain control of the situation, decided to cut adrift the last of the barges – the Cosray 10 with two men aboard.

The Cosray 10's own efforts at anchoring failed and the barge, which was carrying a cargo of steel pipes, came ashore on rocks beneath Natural Arch. The lifeboat was soon on the scene and by anchoring in the deeper water and backing in towards the barge was able to pluck one of the crew to safety.

The lifeboat attempted the difficult manoeuvre again to rescue the second but couldn't get as close and in desperation a line was thrown to the man. The lifeboat crew had intended him to fasten it about his waist and leap into the water but instead he tied the rope to the barge and attempted to cross to the lifeboat one arm over the other.

But his grip failed and he fell into the water and it took a further 10 minutes to bring him inboard. Despite the efforts of the crew he never regained consciousness and was pronounced dead on the lifeboat's return to Brixham.

This was not the end of the drama. The barge broke up and although the cargo of pipes sunk immediately, part of the barge began drifting towards the harbour. The authorities held their breath as the upturned hull narrowly missed the entrance and drifted instead onto Torre Abbey Sands.

It seemed the safer option but continuing storms during the week raised a new peril - that the barge would become, in the hands of the sea, a battering ram to demolish the promenade.

Brixham tugman Ernie Lister attempted to get a line attached but when he failed the authorities called in the fire power of the Royal Marines.

Their task was to puncture its buoyancy and set about their task with enthusiasm, spraying the floating hull with machine gun bullets and launching anti-tank rockets. But the final blow was delivered by the men of the Royal Naval Bomb and Mine Disposal Unit who at low tide blew a giant hole in the hull with a 14 ozs charge of TNT.

The remains of the Cosray 10 remained in the sands of Torre Abbey for some years and became something of a tourist attraction until the salvors finally broke her up.

All that remains now of that tragic vessel is the cargo of pipes scattered like matchsticks around London Bridge and Peaked Tor Cove. They make a curious spectacle on the seabed and it's a popular dive site.

Nature quickly colonised the wreckage and the steel tunnels became perfect homes for a number of species including conger eel.

Indeed it was from this area in 1967 that a six foot conger eel weighing 67lbs was taken on rod and line from the shore. It was a British Record at the time and 30 years on there has only been one larger fish landed. Eels of this size are practically impossible to bring ashore. Angler still try their luck and there are many tales of big fish, hooked but never landed, in this area.

The coastline from Thunder Hole to Natural Arch is generally inaccessible from the shore but the wide platform of rock to the north of the arch can be reached on foot by scrambling down a well-worn track from the coastal footpath. This is Dyer's

Quarry which in 1988 was notified as a site of special scientific interest.

Limestone quarrying in the 19th century exposed a rock face covered in fossils - not the giant ammonites of Charmouth further east but corals and other fauna cemented in time since the Devonian period. The quarry is particularly exciting to geologists and fossil hunters because the corals are in their positions of growth - a frozen snapshot of the seabed 40 million years ago.

The fossil record along this entire stretch of coast is outstanding. The rock platforms on Thatcher Rock alone have yielded nearly 50 different species of fossilized marine molluscs

The southerly aspect of Dyer's Quarry and the shelter it affords has encouraged the growth of some living species! In Spring the whole of this part of Torquay's shoreline is covered in the bright yellow flowers of a Mediterranean shrub planted by Victorians in the gardens of their villas but quick to escape into the natural habitat.

Native species such as scurvy weed and rock samphire also flourish in the rocky hollows where their thick juicy leaves can sustain them during the dry summers. Both species are edible, though scurvy weed was more medicinal than samphire which in some parts of Devon is grown commercially.

It may look unappetising and the white flowers smell revolting, but in fact it can be used in salads and as a pot herb.

The northern boundary of Dyer's Quarry is bounded by Saddle or Scrap Rock where two fingers of stone balance precariously. They have been that way for years but not perhaps much longer.

Adjoining strata is on the move exposing a pink underbelly where the sea has stripped away the rock. All nature's sculptures have an ephemeral quality - carved by her and destroyed by her - an art in constant flux.

Saddle Rock marks the boundary of Torquay's natural shoreline. Until we reach the sanctuary of Hollicombe, the seascape has been much altered by the hand of man.

Our first port of call is Peaked Tor Cove which nestles beneath the gardens of the Imperial Hotel and is reached by a Mediterranean style terrace.

Somewhat out of character with the tranquillity here is a Second World War pillbox. This, I understand was more than just a cosy look-out. Stretching from this emplacement was a string of underwater mines in a line to the old gas works at Hollicombe.

Tradition has it that if invasion threatened, it was the responsibility of these sentries to wind in a cable and release the mines from the seabed so they floated on or near the surface.

Thankfully this last line of defence against an invading enemy was never needed and after the war the mines were carefully recovered.

From Peaked Tor Cove we follow a southfacing shoreline rich in flora which thrives in the limestone fissures. The plants which anchor here are hardy types, not adverse to the occasional dunk in the briny when the waves reach up on tip-toe. The thrift or sea pink is the most striking, the dense tufts decorating the shore in summer like pretty cushions.

This shoreline is inaccessible to the public forming as it does the 'garden wall' of Torquay's Five Star Imperial Hotel but a short while on we reach Beacon Cove - the first of Torquay's bathing beaches.

At the turn of the century this was reserved for women only and equipped with eight bathing machines in which polite Victorian ladies would be winched to and from the water.

Among the regulars was a vivacious Torquay girl who would become known the world over as crime writer Agatha Christie.

Until 1923 Beacon Cove was also the site of Torquay's lifeboat station from where the boat was launched in traditional manner. The building became a council cafe until its demolition in the 1970s.

At low tide a clutter of weed strewn boulder stretch out to sea. This is the line of a ruined stone pier that extended as far as the Mill Stones, two pinnacle rocks that lie about 100 yards offshore. It was swept away in the great storm of 1859 but its foundations provide a rich haven for underwater life.

■ **Beacon Cove in Victorian times with the original Imperial Hotel overlooking.**

A PORT IN A STORM

Torquay Harbour

BEACON Cove marks the boundary of Torquay's natural shoreline.

Until we reach Corbyn Head the landscape is torn and dissected by reclamation, piers and breakwater. It is only by returning to the earliest paintings of Torquay do you grasp the original form of this natural inlet, its rocky creek, marshes and fishermen's cottages clinging to the steeply rising hillside.

Only the cliffs follow the original shoreline of Torquay Harbour. The trail of buildings which throng the harbour are built on land stolen from the sea.

Although Torquay is now the biggest town in Torbay it was the last to develop. Harbours at Livermead, Paignton and Brixham have greater antiquity than those that shelter the pleasure boats and cruisers in Torquay today.

Tradition has it that the first quay built here was erected by Sidmouth fishermen to avoid paying fees at other harbours. It is first recorded in a picture painted in 1680 which shows a single southern arm constructed on a site off Victoria Parade.

The rest of the harbour at that time would, at low tide, have been an expansive beach funneling gradually up the course of the river Fleet. The river now lies culverted under the town centre street which bears it name emerging in a torrent from the harbour wall below Vaughan Parade

By 1800 this single quay had grown a northern arm providing even better shelter and with the fishing industry expanding rapidly resources seem to have been found to extend it further creating what we now know as the inner harbour. The cobbled slip at the back of the harbour and parts of South Pier date from 1806.

For many years the antiquity of South Pier was illustrated by old cannons set into the harbour wall for use as mooring bollards.In 1974 the local authority decided they were too valuable to remain there and the five guns were removed to be properly restored. Two were found to date from the 17th century. Some of the guns were remounted on replica gun carriages and are now on show in Berry Head fort.

Throughout the 19th century Torquay expanded rapidly and the next project to shape Torquay's shoreline was the linking of Torquay harbour with Torre Abbey and Livermead.

For centuries the only way travel between these two parts of the borough was over the top of Waldon Hill, so in 1840 engineers decided to build a road along the base of the cliffs. It was a massive

■ An early painting of Torquay harbour, approximately 1800, when two primitive piers were built off the shore below Park Hill.

■ The inner harbour at high tide in the 1920s.

and expensive job but these were the days of tolls and the builders soon recovered their investment.

Torquay harbour was much painted by Victorian artists but the modern observer is left somewhat confused by the regular featuring of a bare hilltop above what is now Haldon Pier.

Huddled beneath in many of the paintings is a small shipyard owned by William Shaw which although lying outside the harbour at that time had its own slipway from which vessels up to 180 tons were launched.

This landscape is unrecognisable today because in 1870 engineers quarried away the hill, to provide stone for what is now Haldon Pier.

On what was left of Beacon Hill developers built the celebrated Marine Spa, a leisure complex complete with pool, ballroom and sunlit conservatory where Victorian polite society could while away the hours.

It was demolished in the early 70s to make way for an entertainment complex called Coral Island. Despite winning design awards at the time for its clever use of concrete, it could not make its way commercially and in 1997 that too was demolished.

Haldon Pier provided a new southern arm to Torquay Harbour and opened up the possibility of creating a fully protected outer harbour. In 1895 this was achieved with the opening of Princess Pier.

She took five years to build at a cost of £10,000 and was named after Princess Louise, Queen Victoria's daughter who laid the foundation stones.

The completion of the pier and the opening of Princess Gardens nearby must have seemed to the Victorians a suitable civic achievement to end the century. Britain was at its most self-confident with rising living standards and technological breakthroughs effecting the lives of even the poorest.

When Princess Pier was opened in July 1895, 9,000 people turned out to see it. Sightseers were charged tuppence to walk the pier which was decked in lights - the first Torquay illuminations.

One commentator described the scene as a 'chapter from fairyland'.

'The thousands of coloured lamps blending with the Chinese lanterns and flying bunting, together with the strains of the Royal Italian and Torquay bands combined to make the evening one to be remembered in the annals of the borough.'

The pier has seen many changes since then.

The hall, built at the end of the pier for concerts, later became a roller skating rink and then the Island Bar. This was destroyed by fire in 1974 when a workman's blow torch set light to a wooden panel and a strong breeze fanned the flames.

The main structure remains however, a dignified monument to the energy of our civic forefathers. By the turn of the century they had shaped modern Torquay. Where waves once broke in unfettered freedom at the base of cliffs they had laid roads and gardens, built piers and concert halls, strung fairy lights over the dark water. Music and merriment had drowned out the ancient sigh of the sea.

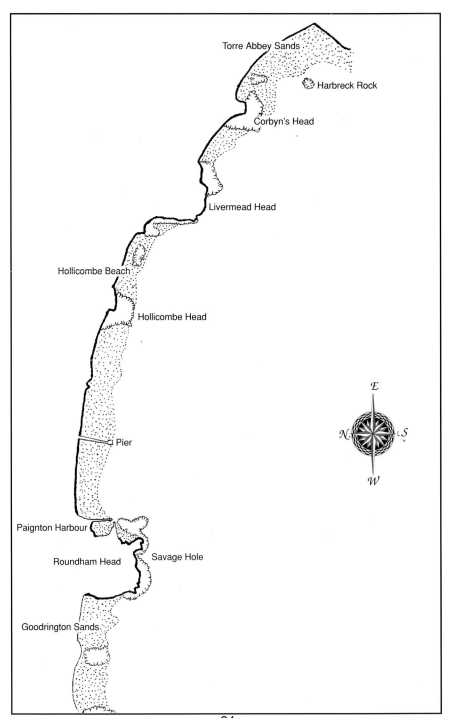

Torre Abbey Sands

Harbreck Rock

Corbyn's Head

Livermead Head

Hollicombe Beach

Hollicombe Head

Pier

Paignton Harbour

Roundham Head

Savage Hole

Goodrington Sands

THE SHALLOWS
Torre Abbey, Livermead and Hollicombe

I have two differing images of Torre Abbey Sands. One is a hot August day when crowds throng the beach and every inch of the concrete lido is lined with sunbathers.

The sea is tamed and the smallest children enjoy the shallows.

The other is at the height of an easterly gale when mountainous waves breach the seawall sending columns of white water over the road.

Then Torre Abbey Sands is a cauldron of reflecting and colliding waves - both terrifying and fascinating.

Torre Abbey has drawn admirers for centuries. Indeed, the monks were the first obvious settlers of Torquay choosing the level ground just inland as the site of their monastery the ruins of which still survive.

The landscape we know today was completed when the sea road was built around the headland of Rock Walk and extended to Livermead.

Engineers have fought a constant battle to preserve their gains against the invading sea. Modern materials and techniques ensure that these days the seafront is merely at risk from flooding not wholesale destruction as witnessed during the 19th century.

The storm of 1859 was

■ A hot day on Torre Abbey in 1926.

■ Atrocious weather in 1938 caused extensive damage and flooding along Torquay seafront as these graphic pictures illustrate.

particularly damaging. It washed away whole sections of Torquay seafront, wrecked the harbour and dumped tons of sand and rubble on Torre Abbey Meadows.

The rogue storm was a south easterly which sustained its barrage for three days. Initially the sea wall which protected the Torquay Road held its own but the first high tide soon undermined it. Breaches were widened with every swell and soon the Meadows were submerged six feet deep.

The safest vantage point was the high ground beside the Spanish Barn and here crowds gathered to watch the destruction.

'As far as the eye could see,' wrote one commentator, 'Nothing could be seen but huge rollers 20 feet high advancing shoreward. Only a faint line here and there indicated where the road once stood.

'From the Spanish Barn a remarkable spectacle; the sea dashing up against the sea wall and then shooting 30 feet before falling onto the Meadows beneath the line of elm and ash.'

The wooden toll house that used to stand at the Livermead end of Torre Abbey Sands was wrenched from its foundations and swept inland. Livermead Road itself was obliterated.

It was the same story around Torquay Harbour. South Pier was swamped and buildings used by the Steam Packet Company carried away. The breakwater from Beacon Cove was reduced to rubble.

Such stories are reminders of the awesome power of wind and sea when they conspire against our fragile defences.

The sea in such a mood seems wilful, bending its back purposefully against neat walls and breakwaters, seeking out a weakness.

Deep in the sand of Torre Abbey is buried a reminder that the sea does not always return to the neat limits we try to impose upon it.

Ten thousand years ago the great glaciers of the ice age began to melt and sea levels around rose dramatically flooding low lying land.

The petrified forest at Torre Abbey is evidence of this sudden invasion.

It can be discovered at the lowest of Spring tides when the water retreats almost as far as Harbreck Rock.

Look for dark areas in the sand where clay lies only a few inches below the surface; on some occasions, particularly after a heavy storm the clay may be completely exposed. This is the seam in which is preserved tree stumps and roots pickled the day the sea came in and never went out.

Outcrops of this fossilised forest are also exposed occasionally at Broadsands and Goodrington and probably at underwater sites all round the shallow bay.

And it isn't just rotting wood which is preserved. Fishermen have been known to dredge up deer antlers, and even flint arrow heads have been discovered, belonging to the stone age men who once roamed these forests.

Today it is sun and sea which draws most people to Torre Abbey Sands. At the height of summer the beach resembles a congested waterhole where crowds compete for every yard.

As a child I enjoyed many such days but now the real pleasure is wandering alone along the pebble dappled sands on a winter's afternoon with the tide at my heels savouring the silence.

IF you walk towards the western end of Torre Abbey Sands you reach Corbyn Beach, a small cove which seems to collect more than its share of rotting seaweed.

At low tide a shallow line of foundation stones running parallel with a rocky gully indicates the remains of an ancient quay. This may date back to the time when the medieval abbey was Torquay's main habitation and the stream that is today channelled and culverted under the main road formed a muddy creek through salt marsh and sand dunes.

The old pier probably served as the Abbey's jetty where everything from French wine to papal emissaries could be landed. It is almost certain that the Spanish prisoners captured during the Armada were brought ashore here before being marched up the abbey causeway, now Kings Drive, to imprisonment in

■ Mitre Rock photographed by Ensor in 1927 when it was a popular place to clamber. The Grand Hotel is in the background and unlike the rock - still standing!

28

what we now call the Spanish Barn.

Torre Abbey monks and their lay brothers were also among the first to fish the waters of Torbay having been granted rights in the original charters and fishing boats no doubt continued to use this convenient quay long after the abbey's dissolution in the 16th century.

But its exposed position would have made it difficult and expensive to maintain and as Torquay Harbour developed, this ancient quay fell into ruin.

Corbyn Beach has seen its fair share of wrecks over the years, the most serious just inside the headland where in 1916 the trawler Girl Edith went aground. The sea was so rough the lifeboat could not be launched and two lives were lost.

As we approach Corbyn Head we greet a new geology. Since our exploration began we have followed a predominately limestone landscape characterised by steep cliffs and sharp offshore rocks. Now the coastline softens to a succession of low headlands and expansive beaches - the Torbay of red clay and sandstone.

Corbyn Head is the first knuckle in the hand, formed thousands of years ago when desert conditions in Devon laid down great deposits of sand and debris in soft horizontal layers.

These layers create a fascinating cliff face at Corbyn Head where the different coloured deposits can be read like the rings of a tree.

Erosion is rapid here. From seaward Corbyn Head is hollowed by seacaves which engineers have bandaged with boulders and cement to prevent their collapse.

This was once the location of Mitre Rock, a spectacular natural arch as celebrated in its time as Natural Arch on the opposite shore.

It was a pyramid shaped stack about 20 feet high chiselled away from the adjoining headland over centuries and pierced by an ample tunnel through which the adventurous could clamber.

It was an attractive feature, but nature is no respecter of elegance and in the 1950s a succession of storms reduced it to rubble. All that remains now of Mitre Rock is a crumbling base of stone.

Tucked inside the headland is another stack in rapid retreat. Old photographs show that this sandstone tower was once a substantial island capped with soft turf and scrub. Now it is whittled away to nothing more than a bare rock - vulnerable to every gale.

This shrinking line of defence once sheltered Hart's boat yard but no doubt as the rock was stripped away the shipwrights abandoned it. The last boat to be built here was the sailing lugger Hazy Morn.

The headland itself is an expanse of grass but during the Second World War it was the site of Torquay's main coastal battery. Equipped with 4.7 inch guns its task was to defend the beaches to the south from invasion. Although the guns were never fired in anger, six men lost their lives here in August 1944 when a practice shoot went disastrously wrong and a shell exploded in the breach of number 2 gun. The Home Guard and Royal Artillery victims are buried in Hero's Corner of Torquay Cemetery.

If the old quay on Torre Abbey served the medieval monastery, then the ruined pier at Livermead served the people of Cockington. Although the village lies a mile inland, the valley that cradles the ancient settlement descends to the sea here through soft clays cut by a tumbling stream. Cockington and Livermead were linked by a track and the harbour became an important part of the village's economy.

The remains of the pier are clearly visible, especially on a low Spring tide when the huge foundation stones, cut from the surrounding rock, are revealed. A defensive arm of stacked slabs extends from Livermead Head while on the Torre Abbey side a free standing quay some 30 feet by 15 feet is definable.What we now call Institute Beach was four centuries ago a small protected harbour.

When it was built is unknown but a bird's eye view of Torbay drawn in 1662 shows the pier with boats tied-up alongside. Being part of the Manor of Cockington its construction and maintenance could have been overseen by the Lord.

We know the Cary family, the local gentry, were fishing here from the 14th century thanks to accounts which still survive.

The Carys had a boat at Livermead Sands and for this a rope and oars were bought in 1439 - more money was paid out for the salting and drying of fish.

Certainly the villagers of Cockington would have made good use of the quay. Records show that seine nets were a common possession among the villagers who could earn a reliable living from the annual harvest of herring and pilchards.

While seine nets could be used in shallow water and the catch brought ashore by men hauling from the beach drift nets were used to snare fish further out. This tangle net hung below floats and was set in the midst of shoals.

To fish accurately boatmen were often directed by a man on the shore. For this purpose a huer's or caller's hut was sometimes built from where a watch could be kept for approaching shoals.

Throughout the Westcountry numerous small harbours were built to exploit the herring and pilchard fishery and there is little doubt that the old quay at Livermead also served this purpose.

It's decay goes unrecorded but it certainly lasted longer than the pier below Torre Abbey. The storms of the 18th century probably saw to its destruction leaving the Cockington fishermen little option but to launch off the beach. An engraving of Livermead in 1830 shows a fishing smack coming directly ashore with little protection from a strengthening easterly breeze.

From the public access to Institute Beach it is possible to scramble across huge platforms of rock to reach the base of Livermead Head.

Here the sandstone cliffs of Torbay reach a dramatic height where the bone of the land is sliced vertically as if by a cleaver. At their base is a chaos of rubble and rockpools and huge seacaves hollowed by the waves.

Rock pigeons love these gloomy retreats and other birds such as gulls and fulmars nest on ledges above.

You would think that man would have left this rock tower unmolested but the arrival of houses on this headland tempted owners to carve their way down to the shoreline. Steps have been dug from the soft stone descending to platforms just above the waves and some have erected ugly concrete huts as private lookouts

But there is a consolation. In Springtime the cliff face is a mass of colour from the wall flowers which have escaped from the confines of clifftop gardens to root in the sandstone crevices.

Rounding the headland we reach Hollicombe Beach which is easily accessible from the main Torquay to Paignton Road through pleasant gardens. But it was not always so. Until the 60s this seascape was dominated by ugly gasworks, and many locals still refer to this now pleasant cove as gasworks beach.

It is a popular area for bird watchers. During the winter months many species migrate south to ride out the worst of the weather on Torbay's sheltered waters.

For many years bird watchers

■ **Livermead in the 1830s when pilchards, herring and mackerel were the main quarry of fishermen.**

were drawn to Hollicombe to view an even rarer visitor. Among the solemn rows of herring gulls was an American - a ringed bill gull which during the 80s made it across the Atlantic and decided to stay.

On tranquil summer days it is difficult to imagine Hollicombe as a storm lashed foreshore but on the night of December 17 1944 this shallow beach was the scene of one of the most dramatic rescues ever by a Torbay lifeboat.

The drama began when the tug Empire Alfred and her tow dragged anchor from her position off Brixham. With the wartime blackout in force the hapless crew of 14 had no idea of their peril until they struck rocks of Hollicombe Point at midnight.

An urgent SOS soon alerted the motor lifeboat George Shee and by 1am Coxswain Fred Sanders had the mast light of the tug in view through the driving rain and spray.

The south easterly storm was reaching its height and mountainous seas were breaking up to 400 yards off-shore - threatening to swamp any vessel which ventured in.

The predicament for Coxswain Sanders was that the tug lay just 50 yards from the shore in a tumult of white water beam on to the swell.

The crew could not be taken off from the sheltered leeside leaving him no option but to edge in on the other. Each time the lifeboat came in huge seas broke over her,

■ An aerial view of Hollicombe Head in the 1950s when the stack Needle Rock was still a feature on the beach.

■ In December 1964 Torbay woke up to find the coaster Northwind beached at Hollicombe. Most were unaware of the dramatic rescue during the night.

but each time she plucked another handful of crew from the wreckage.

It was so shallow that at times the lifeboatmen felt the keel strike bottom but against the odds all 14 crew were rescued.

But that was not the end of it. Another five crew were stranded on the hopper which the tug had been towing and they were in even shallower water.

After dropping the tug crew off in Brixham the lifeboat returned to the scene. Rather than risk damage to his boat by having to back out from the hopper, Coxswain Sanders anchored further out and by paying out 80 fathoms of cable reached the vessel.

Again it was impossible to

reach the leeside so the rescue was attempted in the full force of wind and waves in just eight feet of water. It took 20 minutes to reach four of the men and a further 20 minutes to get the fifth.

For their bravery the six strong crew of the Torbay Lifeboat were honoured by the RNLI, including a rare silver medal for the coxswain.

Twenty years later, in December 1964 another silver medal was won by the coxswain of the Torbay lifeboat in these same treacherous shallows.

The Danish coaster Northwind had been sheltering in the bay when overnight the wind veered to the east and the full power of a Force 10 broke upon the bay. The Northwind dragged anchor and despite the power of her engines she could not stop herself going aground.

The Torbay lifeboat the Princess Alexandra, under the command of Coxswain Harold Coyde, tried time and again to get close enough to take off the crew but the same problem of shallow water encountered 20 years previously made it a hopeless task.

Attention then turned to land based rescuers and volunteer members of the Torbay Coastguard Rescue team who managed to fire a line aboard the vessel and set up a Breeches Buoy pulley system from Hollicombe Beach. Four of the six the crew were winched across the 200 yard gap to safety but not before the lifeline was parted at least once by the seas breaking over the hull of the Northwind.

The captain and mate remained on board but as the weather worsened the decision was made to bring them ashore as well. With the tide rising the Breeches Buoy had to be set up from Hollicombe Head and the men lowered to the rapidly disappearing beach below.

It was to be the last rescue ever made by Breeches Buoy in Torbay and one which won the coastguard auxiliaries a Rescue Shield for their bravery.

Hollicombe Head is another of Torbay's sandstone headlands in rapid retreat. Winter storms pound ceaselessly at the foundations carving deep seacaves which grow until they can no longer support the cliff above. Here, as on other headlands, coastal engineers have shored-up the holes to reduce erosion.

The curtain of rock around the base indicates just how far the headland has retreated and old pictures show features which have long since disappeared including two 20 foot stacks that once stood to the north and south of the headland - Pudding Rock and Needle Rock. The latter survived into the 1960s until the council decided it had become too dangerous and demolished it.

RED SANDS IN THE SUNSET

Preston, Paignton and Roundham

AT Preston we greet the sand, a sweep of crimson shore, almost without feature which at low tide merges seamless with the sea.

But the beach has a linear quality all of its own which contrasts starkly with the right angled cliffs to the north.

This is the landscape of sea and sky that can ease the crowded mind, where nature expresses herself in bold, broad strokes across an open canvas.

Why do we think of the sea as blue when her face reflects a kaleidoscope of colour? On stormy days the sea off Preston swirls blood red with clays washed from the sand and on others a vivid green bruised only by passing clouds.

It is a view which draws the thoughtful, who walk the tide line their worries soothed by the distance and murmur.

During the winter months the, shallow sea off Preston becomes home to ducks and divers which have flown south looking for a milder climate.

My own favourite is the red throated diver, a primitive looking bird with a sharp pointed beak. In

■ Preston Beach in Victorian times. The seawall was built by Paris Singer of Oldway Mansion in 1877.

35

summer when it nests among the lochs of Scotland it has bright red features, but in Torbay we only see its winter plumage which matches the grey weather which billows up the Western Approaches during the dark months of the year.

Larger still is the great northern diver which spends much of its summer fishing the waters of the Arctic.

Other visitors include red necked and Slavonian grebes and the rare black necked grebe, Preston's shallow water providing its only regular wintering site in Devon.

These grebes will appear as bobbing black shapes that routinely disappear from view only to reappear in a circle of water many yards away.

Sea ducks also enjoy the shelter. Here you will find eider, long-tailed duck and the red breasted merganser, which like the grebes dive frequently for fish.

Late summer is also a time for some rare visitors as birds begin their long migration south to escape the British winter. You may be lucky enough to see terns working the shallows diving below the turning swell to feed on sandeels and brit. These elegant birds, streamers trailing, carve the air like scythes as they scour the waves.

MANY of those who walk the strand along Preston and Paignton beach during the winter time would no doubt love to join these migrants' flight to gentler climes.

This stretch is the most exposed in the bay and when the wind rises from the east there is no shelter from the sand and spray flung like hail across the beach.

The only consolation is the spectacle, unsurpassed at the height of a gale. As far as the eye can see, the waves advance like battalions of an army. As the water shallows they reach forward like swordsmen raising their weapons for a final charge.

The battle for Paignton beach has an order and symmetry, different to the squabbling white water which surrounds the headlands.

Easterly storms on Paignton beach rake the sand, digging out shells which litter the shore. Fish can also be casualties, their carcasses quickly attracting the attention of hungry gulls.

The one feature which interrupts the sweep of the bay is Paignton Pier. It has few aesthetic qualities, the buildings which stretch along its length resembling cheap warehousing.

But it wasn't always so. When built in 1878 the only building was a fine pavilion perched on the end reached through a procession of wrought iron arches hung with ornate gas lanterns. The interior of the pavilion was elegantly decorated and fitted with a moveable stage - musical equipment included an organ, harmonium and grand piano. In 1881 a billiard room was also built beside it completing an island of Victorian sophistication, the gaiety of which must have carried far over the water on still summer evenings.

These were genteel days when men and women were forbidden to swim together. Men had to use Preston and ladies Paignton beach along which they paddled and swam from brightly painted bathing machines.

The pier seemed to flourish until a disastrous fire in 1919. The dry timber, covered with new paint and tar, burned furiously and with such intensity that the non-flammable contents of the pavilion, including the organ and piano, fell through the floor into the sea. Parts of the deck further along the pier had to be removed to stop the fire spreading the entire length. Decking was also removed during World War Two as an anti invasion precaution.

Today the most exciting feature of the pier is the ironwork which

■ Punch and Judy have been a tradition on Paignton beach since Victorian times. This crowd were photographed by Ensor in 1927 after the fire had destroyed the pavilion.

■ So hot they needed umbrellas! Paignton beach at the turn of the century.

stitches this Victorian artefact to the seabed.

The falling tide exposes baskets of mussels clinging to the support, so firmly even the most violent storms cannot dislodge them. A small boat can paddle amongst these living piles and explore the marine life which has made much of this solitary anchorage along a mile of shifting sand.

Time travellers would record an ever changing scene along Paignton's seafront. Thousands of years ago the headlands of Roundham and Hollicombe were far more prominent with the beach set much further inland, but the streams which drain out through Victoria and Queen's parks silted up the shallow bay and turned it into salt marsh.

The old town of Paignton grew up on the solid ground to the west, now almost a mile inland, while the wetland provided rough grazing and reeds for basket making. The pier was isolated, surrounded by just a handful of cottages and an inn where visiting sailors were encouraged to pass the evening rather than disturb the locals.

It was not until Victorian engineers built the seawall from Preston to Roundham that the marshland was steadily reclaimed, most recently on the edge of Victoria Park where the library now stands.

But the sea is never far below the surface. On high Spring tides residents who live around the seafront can feel the dampness in their basements and some have had to install pumps to stop their houses flooding. At times Paignton Green is undoubtedly

■ Paignton Harbour at the turn of the century when the terrace in Roundham Road was being built.

below sea level, only the high embankment preventing flooding. It is many years since Paignton's sea defences were breached, but they have been in living memory when high tides and an easterly storm conspired to flood the seafront.

Paignton was once the largest settlement in Torbay and its harbour has a long history. It flourished in the 16th and 17th centuries but by the year 1800 had fallen into disrepair.

The presently harbour owes much to the investment of the Paignton Harbour company which completed its work in 1850. It was always a shallow harbour, and like the ruined quay at Livermead provided a shelter for fishing boats and, as the tourist trade grew, for pleasure craft.

■ **Ensor had some fun with the faces in the rocks when he took this picture at Roundham Head.**

ROUNDHAM Head watches over the waters of Torbay like an old fisherman with his eye on the weather.

The cliffs rise suddenly from the expanse of Paignton beach to form a craggy brow and from here most of the bay is visible.

The shoulder of land rises gently at first craddling the picturesque Fairy Cove, hunching to its greatest height to the south where the headland glowers over Goodrington.

Here the sandstone forms huge buttresses set deep into the cliffs, their ridges eroded into fantastic shapes which to the imaginative resemble numerous faces staring over the waves.

The nooks and crannies of the headland provide ideal nest sites for seabirds such as lesser black backed gulls and fulmars and landlubbers such as rock pigeons which find this isolated spot ideal. Kestrels are often seen here hunting along the rough margins of the headland and in early summer rearing their young on the rock ledges.

At the base of the cliffs the waves pound relentlessly seeking out weakness in the sandstone like sappers at castle walls. Where they can squeeze in they gnaw away at the rock creating sea caves and then, just as they reach architectural brilliance, bring the whole edifice crashing down.

A pattern of reefs extend from Roundham Head like fingers ready to snatch at passing ships. Many have foundered here over the years and although the hulls have long rotted away divers still retrieve barnacle covered artifacts from the sandy gullies.

One of the earliest documented wrecks is of HMS Savage which was lost here in 1762. It must have been a memorable disaster as ever since the small cove below the flats on Roundham Head has been known as Savage Hole.

Another man o' war struck rock in 1804. HMS Venerable, a 74 gun warship was wrecked following a bizarre sequence of events which started with the loss of a man overboard while hauling the anchor. A boat was launched to retrieve him but this was overturned.

While efforts were made to save them, no one realised that in the darkness they were drifting towards the southern reefs of Roundham Head. On seeing the danger desperate efforts were made to tack out to sea again but to no avail in the strengthening easterly.

As she went ashore 500 sailors feared for their lives - the masts were cut in an effort to form a bridge into the shallows, but they fell to seaward, leaving the rescue to be performed by other ships in the vicinity.

By daybreak only the ship's officer and a dozen seamen remained on board the Venerable in loyalty to the captain who refused to leave. Only when the ship's forecastle went under water was he finally persuaded - the

■ It was a stormy night in 1920 when the German torpedo boat V189 went aground on Roundham Head.

40

ship finally breaking in two an hour later.

The valuable cannons were raised a year later by salvors but the remainder of wreckage was left to the mercy of the sea. Divers have searched the wreck site frequently, lying as it does in shallow water, turning up cannon balls, small lead shot and bronze horseshoes used to strengthen the bow of the Venerable.

There are larger remains of a World War One German torpedo boat wrecked here in the 1920.

It is known simply as V189 and was one of two vessels under tow to the breakers when the warp parted in heavy seas. The other went aground at Preston beach and was soon refloated but the V189 struck rock.

The Torquay lifeboat, powered then by sails and oars was launched to rescue the three man crew as was the Brixham motor boat. The seas were so big however that at one point the latter overturned, losing a man overboard. Although the lifeboatman was recovered neither boats could get anywhere near the wreck where the crewmen were stranded.

It was left to the shore-based coastguards to shoot a line aboard and winch the crew to safety

Salvors have stripped the vessel of her valuables over the years, most recently in the 50s when her boilers were raised, but the ribs and some sheets of metal remain - about 200 yards to the south of the beach.

At least two other items lie beneath the waves off Roundham.

Two signal guns went over the cliff one night when the rockface gave way - valuable finds for someone prepared to don snorkel and mask and search the boulders which litter the base of the cliffs.

The promise of sunken valuables has drawn many divers to the Roundham wreck sites over the years. One of the most industrious was Jimmy Thorpe who used to dive the area in the 1930s in a traditional diver's helmet connected to a surface air pump. Most of the V189's bronze and brass was brought ashore by him.

The sea is no preserver of history. Any vessel unlucky enough to founder in the shallow water around Roundham is soon pounded to pieces. Every now and then, however a tantalising remnant is recovered like the flint-lock firing system of an ancient cannon found recently believed to belong to HMS Savage.

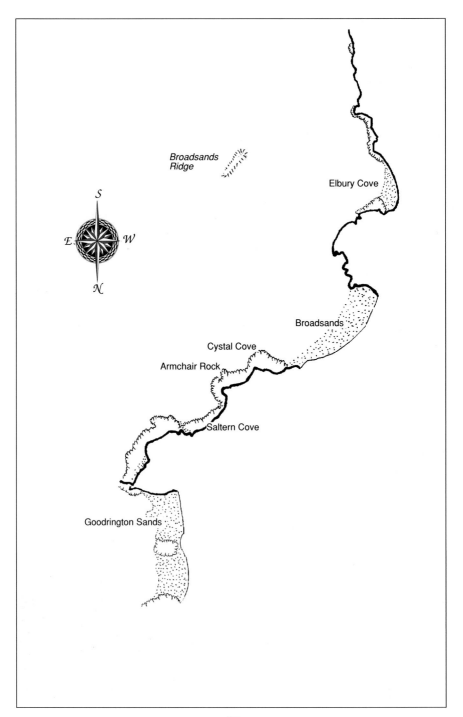

Broadsands
Ridge

Elbury Cove

Broadsands

Cystal Cove

Armchair Rock

Saltern Cove

Goodrington Sands

S

E W

N

ROCK AND A HARD PLACE

Goodrington to Broadsands

From the vantage point of Roundham Head a zig-zagging path descends to Goodrington's promenade. This pleasant short cut to the beach was chiselled from the cliff face by council contractors in 1938 and forms a sheltered south-facing garden.

During the 19th century Goodrington beach must have been an eerie place for the area that we now know as Young's Park was a graveyard surrounded by marshes.

It served a Napoleonic hospital which stood on a small area of raised ground between the two beaches and parts of which are now incorporated into a seafront pub.

Holidaymakers picnicing there have only one clue as to what lies in the sandy soil beneath them - a single remaining grave stone belonging to Major Thomas Hill.

The hospital was converted in 1800 from an existing house on the site, the origins of which are unknown, and remained in operation until about 1816 when the war in Europe ended. Patient numbers averaged around 30 tended by a surgeon, a matron

■ Goodrington before the rock walk was built into the cliff and the promenade created.

43

and two nurses.

They were mostly sailors and Royal Marines although men of the 88th regiment based at Berry Head were also treated there. Typical ailments were flux, hernias, ulcers and, most common of all, venereal disease.

How many men were buried in the adjoining graveyard during this short period is unknown but as the area was consecrated it seems likely other bodies were interred there during the early part of the 19th century. By the end of it however waves had breached the sea wall and were exposing the graves. A storm in 1917 revealed a number of bones and the back of the beach and the current sea defence is at least 20ft further inland than they were 100 year ago.

The history of Goodrington goes back much further however and it is possible that the raised sandstone ledge upon which the seafront buildings stand had much earlier inhabitants, standing as it did at the boggy mouth of Clennon Valley.

There is evidence of stone age and bronze age settlement further inland and over the years, metal detectors have turned up a number of interesting finds in the sands including Roman coins and a Viking broach.

In 1883 three pewter flagons were found, one of which was identified as 4th century AD, and a fourth was uncovered by a metal detector in 1979.

But if you are looking for treasure at Goodrington today, I suggest you leave the metal detector at home and enjoy some of the natural wonders that

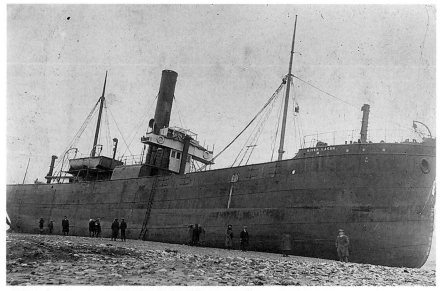

■ Some visitors to Goodrington would rather not be there. This was the River Lagan that went ashore in 1927. She was successfully refloated on the next high tide.

uncover at low tide.

The sweep of terracotta sand which stretches towards the horizon may appear a lifeless zone but the occasional hole reveals the presence of creatures which flourish beneath the sand where neither waves nor predators can reach them

Scoop with your hands around one of these holes and you may uncover a razor fish, a shellfish so named because it is shaped like the an old cut-throat razor, as well as other kinds of clams.

You may happen upon a sea potato, a sea urchin which resembles a tennis ball, and which survives by siphoning plankton down a star shaped depression in the sand.

A lifeless ball it may seem but rest the urchin on the sand and the tiny bristles will begin to claw the body beneath the surface.

The succession of holiday beaches and rock gardens which characterise the Paignton coastline is broken by a wild and difficult shoreline at Saltern Cove.

This fascinating stretch of coast is actually three rocky beaches separated by small headlands easily negotiated at low tide.

After the promenades and noisy sideshows of Goodrington, this unspoiled stretch comes as a welcome relief for those who relish rock pools and gullies, where the only music is the gurgle and splash of sea.

Saltern Cove is a landscape in turmoil where two great rock systems collide in unhappy union.

■ **Goodrington photographed from Roundham Head in 1909. The graveyard behind the beach has already disappeared and is being used for grazing.**

45

The white of the limestone fuses with Torbay's red sandstone piling agony on the strata which ruptures this way and that. Where there is weakness the sea has carved deep gullies leaving harder, crystalised outcrops exposed.

Geologists get very excited by the rock formation here and it is a Site of Special Scientific Interest for this reason. But even the amateur can't help notice the great upheavals of pre-history which have left their mark here like no other stretch of Torbay's coast

The cliffs vary from knuckle-hard strata, folded and compressed into tortuous patterns to belly-soft clay in constant flux.

It is down one of these clay shoots that we reach the northern most bay of the Three Beaches headland. The council has provided scaffolding steps to reach the shore which saves a scramble through waist-high undergrowth.

Below the tide line the bay is a shamble of 'fruit cake' boulders - limestone rubble welded in sandstone 'cement' by forces which also shaped the kelp covered ridges which run out to

■ **This wreck uncovered at low tide at Broadsands some years ago may still lay beneath the sand. She was probably one of those wrecked in the great storm of 1866.**

46

sea here for hundreds of yards.

There is further revelation around the next promontory where the sweep of Saltern Cove begins. The scramble over the rocks is worth it if only to examine the curious intrusion in the bedrock which, after centuries of erosion protrudes from the cliff face like the rim of sailor's cap.

On reaching the beach, notice the sand underfoot. Unlike Goodrington's ground red sandstone, the sand here is mainly pulverised shell, evidence of the shellfish which thrive in Saltern Cove's sunlit waters. Over 60 species have been recorded here one reason why this area is also a marine nature reserve.

Further on are two other features to admire.

Armchair Rock stands alone like a resilient molar in a tired jaw. It shelters a tiny beach of crushed white shells skirted by boulders. On a calm day light dances in the shallows drawing the swimmer into its cool embrace.

The difficult scramble over rock will also bring you to the site of crystal cave. This was once a major attraction and many a picture was taken of its star studded interior.

But whether at the hands of men, keen to carry-off souvenir crystals, or the clawing sea, the cave has now collapsed and all that remains is a narrow fissure penetrating deep into the cliff face.

But it's still impressive, fist-sized crystals line its inner wall like teeth; hunt around at low tide and you will discover examples prised from the rock face.

From here it is only a short walk to the cliff top path which takes you to Broadsands. Alternatively you can continue to follow the shoreline beneath the cliffs where the rock patterns of Saltern Cove are repeated ever more dramatically. Be careful though, the going is slippery and a rising tide can cut you off.

Which ever way you walk - the reward is the wide, firm expanse of Broadsands beach which at low tide uncovers for hundreds of yards.

It's a quiet inlet which before the car parks were built was backed by sea marsh and reed beds. Families crowd the beach here in the summer enjoying the safe shallow water - unaware that it is a notorious wreck site.

Ships torn from anchorages off Brixham were inevitably swept this way and over the centuries the soft but crushing embrace of Broadsands claimed many a vessel.

The worst incident was in 1866 when no fewer than 13 vessels founded during a snow storm. It was the night of January 11 when a gale, from which ships had been sheltering, veered suddenly catching around 100 vessels, from schooners to fishing smacks, at anchor.

Ships were blown ashore along a stretch of coast from Brixham to Goodrington - an old photograph shows Brixham harbour bobbing with splintered hulls - but low tide at Broadsands provided the greatest spectacle.

Here vessels had been swept

■ A rural view of Broadsands before the surrounding fields were covered in housing. Seven Quarries and Brixham are in the distance.

high up the beach while the wreckage of many others lay strewn along the strand. It was a scene of utter devastation but incredibly the loss of life was less here than at other places because coastguards managed to fire lines to the stranded crews.

The 50 sailors pulled through the surf at Broadsands were the lucky ones. Dozens of others shipwrecked beneath steep cliffs at Elbury and Saltern Cove had no chance to scramble ashore to safety.

It is estimated that of 100 vessels at anchor in the bay that winter's night, 80 were wrecked and 100 lives lost. Twenty nine bodies were buried in a mass grave in St Mary's churchyard, Brixham and others at Goodrington.

Many of the ships wrecked at Broadsands were refloated but those which were beyond repair were burned on the sands. For many years the timbers of these ships were exposed at low water and there is every reason to believe that some ancient keels from these and other vessels still lie buried in the silt.

In the mid-1980s these waters were surveyed by divers using a magnetometer – following up rumours that a ship of greater antiquity and value than any which foundered in 1866, was located there. Whether anything was found remains a mystery.

If you stand on Broadsands beach and look towards Brixham breakwater you may notice crab pots bobbing offshore. These mark the location of the Broadsands ridge, one of Torbay's few offshore reefs which forms a crowded habitat for marine life.

The ridge is of sandstone and emerges like giant vertebrae from the sea bed in an approximate line from Broadsands to Seven Quarries. It rises no more than a couple of fathom but the cover it provides is a paradise for predators. Conger eels up to 40lbs have been caught here.

Wherever there is cover fish will hide. Not far from the ridge lie two ship's anchors locked together in a cradle. It is the home of a solitary bull huss - the perfect detached dwelling for such a greedy dogfish!

Further out to sea there is little of interest - just a monotonous expanse of mud and silt so deep you can plunge your arm in and it will disappear up to the elbow. It is a lifeless zone where currents are subdued and nature has never spread her seeds.

Even at the height of an easterly gale little disturbs the deep, silent water.

But there are discoveries to be made in this underwater desert. After the war trawlers often snagged the debris of battle strewn around the ocean floor. It was a menace and valuable tackle was regularly lost. Over time the wreckage was logged and trawlers learned to fish clear of the snags.

Shallow wrecks were soon explored by divers eager to identify them. Off Berry Head an American airforce Fortress bomber was located and two engines and four propellers raised.

The greatest excitement, however, followed the discovery of a twin engined Avro Ansun right in the middle of the bay on a line between Hopes Nose and Berry Head.

The plane went down in 1951 when its port engine failed. The three crew, who had been on a training flight, escaped unhurt.

She lay undetected in 90 feet of water until 1975 when the Devon Aircraft Recovery Team found her and began the delicate operation of raising her to the surface.

The team originally planned to lift her in one go with the help of buoyancy bags but a sudden change of weather forced a re-think. They got the port engine first and then returned, when the weather had settled, for the rest.

The fuselage was filled with thick mud and in time she would have disappeared into the ooze to be lost forever.

The Ansun is now preserved in a warehouse - neatly dissembled and packed into boxes, awaiting the day when a new generation takes an interest in this hapless workhorse of the air.

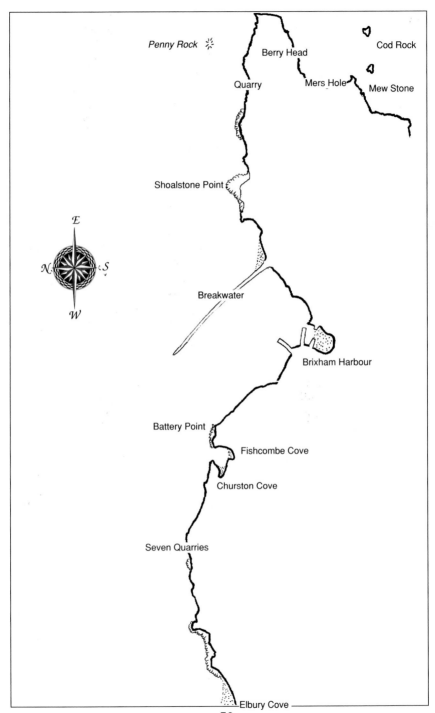

Penny Rock

Berry Head

Cod Rock

Quarry

Mers Hole

Mew Stone

Shoalstone Point

𝓔
𝓝 — 𝓢
𝓦

Breakwater

Brixham Harbour

Battery Point

Fishcombe Cove

Churston Cove

Seven Quarries

Elbury Cove

SECRET COVES AND HARBOUR LIGHTS

Elbury Cove to Brixham Harbour

BROADSANDS is the last of Torbay's wide sandstone beaches. As we walk south the land hardens and cliffs rise quickly from the foreshore, sheltering small steeply shelving coves of wave-ground pebbles.

At Elbury the limestone beach dazzles like coral sand in vivid contrast to the lush green woods which surround it. This is a magical place where on quiet days the whispering sea conjures dreams of foreign idylls.

But expect no peace if your visit coincides with peak season when the waters of Elbury become a race circuit for power boats. Then the tranquil scene is disrupted by sudden waves and revving outboards.

The best time to visit Elbury is on a Spring day when the beach has been washed clear by winter storms and the debris of summer swept away. Then the water is icy clear and the strengthening sun plays in the shallows.

Divers are drawn to Elbury to observe an interesting natural phenomena- submerged freshwater springs which bubble up from the seabed about 100 yards offshore. Underwater they form saucer shaped depressions in the sand and as the water bubbles up it shimmers - an optical effect created by the mixing of different water

densities. It's an indication again of the peculiar geology of this stretch of coast.

For over a century Elbury Cove was the private beach of the Lords of Churston and it was they who built the 19th century bathing station that nestles below Marridge Woods. It was reached by a track, or carriage drive, across what is now Churston Golf Course.

It is a curious ruin with many features you would not expect in a simple beach house, like plentiful fireplaces and outbuildings.

Behind it a fine set of granite steps lead down to a stone pier

■ **Bathing station at Elbury Cove as it was in 1927.**

51

and others have been cut from the rock to reach the water's edge. This was surely more than just a summer house.

Old photographs show the building with a thatched roof and a retaining wall sheltering the doors and windows from northerly winds. This has now been undermined by the sea and fallen onto the beach, but a winch survives suggesting that a small slip may also have been in use to brings boats ashore.

Like Broadsands, Elbury has had its fair share of dramas. Boatmen who used to ferry visitors here in the summer earlier this century remember the entrance at low tide being hindered by wreckage - possibly a victim of the 1866 storm.

The coaster Sloman was driven ashore here when she caught fire 25 miles west of Start Point in December 1861. Refloated at high tide, the fire was eventually put out by firemen in Brixham harbour who pumped water in by cutting holes in her sides.

Elbury is the last accessible stretch of coast in this corner of the bay. From here abrupt limestone cliffs rise sharply creating a wilderness shore line known locally as Seven Quarries on account of the extensive quarrying here between 1830 and 1920.

Torbay's limestone was a precious resource and it was easily quarried; millions of tons went for construction, steel production and fertiliser.

Before the advent of superphosphates and guano fertilisers lime was vital to farmers. The stone was excavated, loaded aboard barges moored alongside and then dispersed to thousands of lime kilns for burning. The fine powder that was left was then spread on the land. Lime kilns are still common in Devon, particularly along the estuaries which took supplies directly from Torbay. There are two close by - in the wooded Grove above Churston Cove.

At their height, the Brixham quarries employed hundreds of men who laboured away with picks and crowbars singing as they worked. Visitors recall constant hammering carrying over the water mingling with occasional songs. Now only the wind and sea chorus in this lonely, jagged place.

It is possible to reach the quarries on foot, but step cautiously. The quarrying has created deep chasms and drop-offs and to reach the waterline on foot is a precarious struggle through thick vegetation. Despite the industry which thrived here, nature has quickly reclaimed the cliffs and quarry floors which are now home to many species.

Amongst the sycamore and oak, a pair of buzzards nest. On hot days you will see them drifting on the air currents which rise from the quarry floors keeping a lookout for prey on which to swoop.

Seamen can approach Seven Quarries from the sea without hazard and come alongside in the way the old barges did. There are mooring eyes still holding firm among the crevices through which to slip a line.

■ The age of sail was giving way to steam when Ensor snapped this harbour view of Brixham in 1926.

Scramble into one of the inaccessible quarries in Spring and you will discover a secret garden. Scurvy weed and thrift thrive in the cracks and hollows while further above the breaking sea primroses and campions have found a hold.

Seven Quarries is the wildest stretch of Torbay's coast and it remains inaccessible to all but the fittest explorer.

The coastal path which runs high above the quarries alongside Churston golf course descends steeply to Fishcombe.

The coastline of Torbay is shaped typically by the sea's appetite for sands and clay, the limestone headlands of Berry Head and Hopes Nose increasingly prominent as the red sandstone of Preston and Paignton has retreated.

This process is seen in miniature at Fishcombe where over thousands of years wind and tide have lapped out the softer shales to create an intriguing cove sheltered from almost every direction.

Fishcombe is unusual in that you can approach the sea here through wild countryside unspoilt by housing or holiday park development.

Alight at Churston village and follow the footpath from Bascombe Road through ancient field systems bounded by neat dry stone walls.

Soon you reach the boundary of the Grove, a dense wood which leads down to the beach. The woods are interesting because they are believed to be a remnant of ancient woodland; tell-tale species include wood spurge and small leafed lime. Here to, as mentioned earlier, you will find lime kilns collapsing slowly under the creeping foliage.

You emerge from the damp, shady woods into blinking sunlight and a suntrap of bright limestone pebbles. Churston Cove is the most sheltered in the bay which means that water visibility here is exceptional and you don't need a snorkel and mask to watch the sandeels flashing in the shallows.

I have sat here at night around the embers of a fire and watched the phosphorescence breaking in the waves. Distant splashes and the clunk of oars working in the rollocks take you back to the days when such coves were the favourite haunt of smugglers running their contraband ashore.

Fishcombe Cove is the other side of the woods and during the 19th century it sheltered a shipyard - one of seven such yards which flourished in Brixham as the fishing fleet expanded.

The entrance to Brixham harbour is guarded by Battery Point. As its name suggested the low headland has been a key defence post for centuries none more so than when Nazi invasion threatened. It was from here that the bay was to be defended with weaponry which could strike targets far out in Lyme Bay.

Walk in Battery Point gardens today and you will enjoy a

tranquil retreat where only the breaking sea on the rocks below disturbs the silence, but return to the dark, dangerous days of the Second World War and it was a very different place.

At night searchlights swept the bay as gun crews on constant alert awaited enemy attack. And on the rising land behind the bunkers the crew of the Bofors gun stood by ready to open up on hit and run raiders which often bombed the town.

From the sea it must have looked a formidable defence with barbed wire ringing the shoreline and two great barrels pointing seaward.

The 4.7 inch guns were capable of sending high explosive or shrapnel shells over 10 miles but they were never fired in anger despite the incursion of enemy E-boats into the bay on a number of occasions.

The heavy artillery was supplemented by a 20lb gun trained inshore towards Freshwater Quarry to defend Brixham harbour and there were anti-aircraft guns and rockets on other sites around the headland.

The gun emplacements are now preserved as a major feature of Battery Gardens and with Brownstone at the mouth of the Dart is one of the few complete World War Two defences the public can explore.

The two gun emplacements are still intact as are some of the tunnels which connect them. They now form a pleasant spot to shelter from the wind whilst enjoying views of the harbour.

■ Half tide in Brixham inner harbour in 1925.

Observation points and searchlight emplacements are also preserved nearby.

The concrete defences of World War Two are familiar all along the South Devon coast and little regard has been paid to them as historic sites.

But as the years go on and the war becomes a distant memory, greater interest will be shown by a new generation to these grim monuments of war.

RECLAMATION has transformed the natural contours of Torbay's shoreline, especially Brixham.

If we sailed into Brixham 200 years ago we would barely recognise the harbour stretching as it did a further half mile inland along a narrow, muddy creek well beyond Bolton Cross.

On either side, steep wooded slopes sheltered huddled cottages rising to plateaux of limestone to east and west.

Higher and lower Brixham were separate communities, the names fishtown and cowtown still survive, and a ferry service ran between them.

But smelly creeks have few friends and as the town grew more and more was reclaimed.

The process was speeded by the damming of the creek across its mouth, where the Strand dissects the harbour. It was built centuries ago to harness the ebbing tide for giant mills constructed either end of the valley.

A similar design survives at Stoke Gabriel and although the mill itself has gone, the dam and wheel well remain intact.

This interruption to the natural flow led to a progressive silting up of the creek making reclamation even easier. The old stream was at first channelled but finally culverted erasing the last reminder of the town's muddy vein.

Not quite! In 1955 the remains of a quay wall was discovered under a toy shop at Bolton Cross.

Reclamation has continued apace during the last 10 years. Oxen Cove was the last stretch of natural shoreline to disappear under tons of building rubble, earth, and hardcore and if the Northern Arm plan ever comes to fruition another half mile of shore will also wear a concrete skirt.

It is a visual scar, but marine life soon recolonises the blank walls and transforms them into a dripping collage of colour.

One year I left my boat in the water too long and the hull, once polished to a shine, grew a slimy rug of weeds and clustered shells. Even a sea squirt took up residence. So nature is not shy to cultivate the most barren landscape and blend it with her own.

An alternative, and probably more attractive view of Brixham can be enjoyed at night when darkness has thrown a discreet veil over the ugly shoreline development and the canvas is simplified to splashes of warm colour reflected on an inky sea. For the homecoming sailor it is a welcome sight.

And the fish quay like a flaring

beacon glows the brightest as fishermen working under deck lights prepare for the morning's fish auction or departure on the next tide.

Brixham is distinguishable from Torbay's other harbours as the home to southern England's largest trawler fleet.

This association shapes the character of the harbour which isn't sanitised for the benefit of tourists.

It smells of crab bait and fish guts, diesel and harbour mud - the inimitable smell of the sea familiar since childhood.

I have wandered around the quays late on Christmas Eve when nearly all the fleet is in and the pubs are full of fishermen home for festivities. Around the harbourside, tethered in creaking rafts, is a ramshackle armada of rusting steel dented by swinging gear and battering seas.

It is easy to be romantic about life at sea but it is a comfortless world, a mix of boredom and great physical effort troubled by ever present danger.

Commercial pressure means trawlers put to sea in conditions which pleasure fishermen would never entertain and with ever diminishing catches, trawlermen must travel ever further afield.

Fishing in Brixham has continued since the first inhabitants built their homes in this sheltered creek over 900 years ago.

But it was in the 19th century when the industry took off encouraged by a growing market for fish and new techniques such as beam trawling which allowed nets to scour the bottom.

In 1850 there were 270 trawlers fishing out of Brixham providing work for 1,600 seamen but with increased competition from the North Sea fleets the industry began to decline.

The death knell for the red sailed fishing smack was sounded by the First World War, which left so much wreckage strewn around the seabed that nets were continuously snagged and lost. By 1935 there were only 26 boats left and only six vessels in 1939.

The present revival owes much to the establishment of a fishing co-operative in Brixham in 1965 and a boom in the public's appetite for fish.

But now fishing faces its gravest threat which could see it reduced to little more than a cottage industry. The stark fact is that South West waters have been so intensely trawled in recent years that there are few fish left.

For the moment the trawlermen struggle on and the fish quay retains its fascination for those intrigued by this most ancient of professions.

Like a crucible of endeavour, it is the focus of the harbour, rarely asleep, restless with the noise of gear hoists and sliding fish boxes - the beating heart of the town.

The last great landmark of Brixham is its breakwater built for the practical purpose of protecting the harbour from easterly gales.

For centuries ships have been

tempted into Tor Bay with promises of shelter from prevailing southwesterlies. Brixham is particularly attractive because of the shelter offered by 200 feet limestone cliffs.

But if the wind veers suddenly there is no protection and many sailors have lost their lives in Brixham's beguiling waters.

The breakwater was built to provide at least one area of safe anchorage.

Like most public projects it took years to build. Permission was first granted in 1837 and the first stone laid in 1843 with the help of loans and donations from local people. Money ran out after 1,400 feet and work did not begin again until 1909 when it was extended by a further 600 feet. In 1912 the final thousand feet of breakwater were added giving Brixham harbour its long dreamed of protection.

It's a long walk to the end but an enjoyable one for those who relish the harbour views and savour the sound of the sea.

Inside the breakwater the water is subdued and moves silently among slippery boulders jammed with plastic bottles and cartons from the harbourside takeaways.

Old ropes, bearded with green weed stretch into the murky shallows giving cover to bass and mullet which like to feed on the marine life which flourishes here.

It is a quiet, sheltered place in contrast to the scene the other side of the wall where on windy days reflecting waves churn the sea into a confusion of white water, throwing foam high into the air.

STORMY BUTTRESS
Shoalstone Point and Berry Head

Even at the height of a south westerly gale there is one stretch of Torbay's coast which remains blissfully sheltered, where high cliffs and an easterly aspect offer superb protection from the worst of weather.

This is the shore between Shoalstone Point and Berry Head where you can enjoy quiet water while mountainous seas lash the shore the other side of the point

The shelter here made Shoalstone an ideal site for a swimming pool and thousands of Brixham families have fond memories of summer days spent there.

A sluice gate traps the water at high tide and ensures a good depth throughout the day. Each high tide flushes the pool with fresh water.

But it isn't just water which is trapped behind the sluice gate. Occasionally the dropping tide maroons fish in the pool much to the amusement of bathers.

A few years ago the pool had to be closed when a giant shoal of brit, similar to white bait, filled

■ **An aerial view of Berry Head with the quarry partly in shadow.**

59

the swimming bath giving seabirds an easy meal until the rising tide released them from their imprisonment.

Shoalstone has other attractions. The rocks are strangely patterned; white limestone veined with dark, terracotta sandstone - resembling streaky bacon.

The feature was formed when the original limestone bedrock became fractured and windblown sand flowed into the fissures. Geological upheaval then welded the rocks together. Calcite veins run trough the sandstone adding to the striking pattern

Rockpools, ground by the sea from the limestone platform, collect colourful pebbles which in the bright sun sparkle like caches of precious jewels.

Crab pots a few hundred yards off Shoalstone Point indicate rough ground.

I am often puzzled by how such marks get their names. Within a few hundred yards of the shore are three noted reefs, The Rows, Penny Rock and a mark known as John Hermon's.

Whoever he was he would be delighted to know his favourite fishing spot has been named after him.

Bass, which these days are spoken about in low whispers owing to their rarity and value, can be found here. They used to be plentiful in South Devon waters but over fishing has devastated stocks and a five pound fish is now worth £20 on a fishmonger's slab.

The reef is dissected by a shingle gully and currents which gather pace along Shoalstone trap food here.

In the right conditions big shoals of bass are drawn in and superb fish, up to 10lbs, have been taken by anglers casting from the shore.

THE land is now running out. Our journey around Torbay's coastline which started at Hopes Nose has covered nearly 22 miles and we are, so to speak, on the final tack sailing towards the buttress of Berry Head.

This limestone promontory is Torbay's Cape Horn where currents strengthen and raw westerly winds, funnelled by the headland, raise threatening seas.

So let us linger for a moment in the lee of Berry Head where the quiet waters of the bay are preserved.

This sheltered edge is dominated by the quarry, a huge excavation that only ceased in 1969 at the insistence of conservation groups concerned that the headland may be eaten away.

It was a timely halt. In 1973 Berry Head was declared a nature reserve of national importance.

The quarry is an eerie place where long shadows reach to the water's edge. Tides, which move only sluggishly within the bay, gather pace here and fling flotsam and jetsam from the harbour far out to sea.

At dusk the creepy atmosphere is heightened by the occasional appearance of Britain's largest, and rarest bat, the greater horseshoe.

They live in caves uncovered by

quarrymen in the cliff face and you will certainly know if you've seen one with wing spans of up to 14 inches.

The whole of Berry Head is riddled with caves above and below high water mark. When a swell is running the latter boom and gurgle beneath the quarry floor as waves flood the fissures.

Cavers have explored some of the cracks uncovered by quarrying. There are more than 50 up to 215 metres long with names such as Sweetwater Pot and Shaky Caves. Many are only entered through dangerous sumps which require cavers to hold their breath and swim through flooded sections.

The quarry also gives access to Torbay's most celebrated angling mark - Hairy Ledge, so called because of the dangerous climb needed to reach it.

It is a hazardous clamber and at least one lad has died attempting it but the fishing can be so good that many persist - wisely with the help of a rope.

A cast from here gives you access to the deepest shoreline water in South Devon and the opportunity to land fish normally only taken from boats.

The most exciting was a giant sunfish, the size of my desk, hooked on mackerel gear, seen but never landed.

Basking sharks, dolphins and even a whale have been seen from Hairy Ledge. One friend has related time and again the awesome moment when a sudden gasp of air broke the morning silence, and turning towards the sound watched a giant tail sink below the surface just 50 yards offshore.

FROM the summit of Berry Head our journey round the coast of Torbay reaches its dramatic height.

Our shoreline exploration has for many miles enjoyed a picturesque but limited horizon.

At Berry Head the view explodes to reveal an undiscovered country of new bays and headlands disappearing into the distant west.

Visitors here share the elation of climbers who after much effort attain the ridge and discover new opportunities beyond.

Sea and sky are gigantic, dwarfing to insignificance the boats rounding the headland far below.

This lofty turret with the waters of South Devon at its feet has been a defensive stronghold for thousands of years.

Iron Age man threw up a 30 foot rampart to defend the promontory and the same site was probably used by the Romans; coins and pottery from the period have been unearthed here.

The present forts were built during the Napoleonic wars when the French warmonger threatened invasion. Three forts were planned but building work on the third, above the Berry Head Hotel, was never started.

The northern fort still dominates the headland but only one building survives, that of the guardhouse, now a tearoom.

The Berry Head forts were abandoned in 1825 and the sound of marching troops disappeared from the headland until invasion threatened again in 1940. Both British and American troops were stationed here during the war manning anti-aircraft guns to defend the bay.

Today the stations of war are silent and nature slowly, but relentlessly erases the ugly wounds.

Nature has indeed crowned this headland with many treasures. The limestone bedrock nurtures a habitat unique to Devon where botanists lose themselves for hours pouring over the rich turf.

In Spring yellow rattle cover the northern slopes and white rock roses cluster among the sheltered crags. Bee orchids and pyramidal orchids also flourish away from the main paths providing nectar for rare butterflies like the adonis blue and small pearl bordered fritillary.

Later in the year the purple flower of the autumn squill pushes up through the turf while another rare orchid - autumn ladies tresses can be identified.

One of the delights of Berry Head are the natural turrets of rock which hang almost vertically over the water. Far below a running tide slops and swirls through the sea caves.

One such promontory allows you to view the guillemot colony tucked in beneath the old redoubt of number one fort. The sheltered pool beneath these cliffs is known as Mers Hole to local fishermen, mers being the local name for the

■ **The undiscovered country: looking west from Berry Head.**

penguin-like guillemots which nest on the narrow ledges above it.

Curiously guillemots go by the same name in America - carried into the American vocabulary by West Country settlers no doubt.

The adult guillemots arrive on the cliffs early in the new year. The eggs hatch in the Spring and by June the young birds are ready to leave the nest. There are an estimated 400 birds which nest here and the chicks will leave the security of the cliff ledge for an uncertain life on the sea over a few nights coinciding with the summer solstice.

It's a dramatic event. The chicks wait till dusk and then, responding to some unknown signal, throw themselves from the ledges, featherless wings flapping to no effect. Many actually collide with the rockface as they fall but survive to join their parents in the rising swell. They continue to be nurtured by their parents for many weeks.

Occasionally Berry Head is visited by some outstanding birds such as the gyr falcon which landed here in 1988. This huge predator, hopelessly lost, is normally only found north of Iceland.

It stayed for over a week attracting thousands of bird watchers captivated by its power and magnificence. It fed on jackdaws and pigeons which it would snatch in mid-air between fierce talons.

Birdwatchers were not the only people interested in this rare visitor. Illegal falconers offered up to £50,000 for the capture of the bird; even the warden of Berry Head was approached.

In the Spring you will see the first migrant birds, resting up for a few hours after completing their cross Channel migration. Sand martins and wheatears are among the first soon followed by big flocks of swallows turning cartwheels through the evening sky.

The lighthouse at the end of Berry Head is a natural focal point for visitors. It was built in 1906 and became known as the smallest, highest and deepest light in the British isles! The tower is only five metres high but the light is 58 metres above the water casting a beam across an 18 mile range. It is the deepest light in the world because the optic used to be turned by a weight falling down a 150 ft shaft.

The headland has seen many wrecks over the centuries. Memorable losses include the captured French brig Cerbere which struck rocks in February 1804. She lay in shallow water and her supplies and ten cannons were salvaged.

There was another chance for Brixham wreckers to profit when the John Mermann, on its way from Hamburg to Sierra Leone went aground. Her cargo consisted of coloured handkerchiefs, blue beads and general barter goods for African natives. Relics from her still turn up.

Divers are drawn to rough ground just to the south of Berry Head called the Trawler Dump

where over the years old boats
have been scuttled and debris
dredged from the sea bed in nets,
dropped overboard.

Berry Head is an appropriate
place to end our journey, gazing
over 800 square miles of sea and
coastline, where generations have
stood before.

Wives and children have waited
here hoping for a glimpse of sail
to reassure them of their loved
one's return, soldiers have
watched, adventurers have
dreamed, poets have walked
away inspired. They have come
and gone. Only the sea, ever the
same and yet ever changing,
endures.

*THIS book is dedicated to the memory of my
father who through his great knowledge of
the sea taught me to love and respect it.*